Foreword

This project is a literary and musical collaboration between Toni Morrison and Rokia Traoré, moving across continents, shared and divergent histories, imagined "other worlds," and the darkly resonant, open-ended poetry of William Shakespeare's *Othello*.

Writing from Bamako, in Mali, Rokia Traoré is one of a new generation of African women, a clear and courageous citizen of the world stepping forward into leadership, musical heir to the griot traditions of the Mandean royal courts and the particular alchemy of Malian music that gave birth to the blues in North America. Her music is a rich blend of cross-Atlantic traditions in a distinctly feminine voice.

Toni Morrison has created fiction that imagines, evokes and honors the missing histories of generations whose courage, struggles, achievements, loves, tragedies, fulfillments and disappointments have gone unrecorded, but are still very much with us.

Shakespeare's *Othello* is a permanent provocation, for four centuries the most visible portrayal of a black man in Western art. It is a play seething with innuendo, misinformation, secrets, lies, self-deception, cruelty, and strangely luminous redemption. It has been read by generations as a coded, indirect reference to the coded, indirect layers of justice and injustice that move across racial lines in Western societies. Because the play is so intricate and ultimately disturbing, much of its performance history has reduced it to a kind of puppet show of a brilliant but dangerously mad black man framed by a devil on his left (Iago) and an angel on his right (Desdemona).

What was the reality of Africa for Shakespeare? Did he know any Africans? Clearly the man who called his theater "The Globe" was interested in Africa, and his two "multicultural" plays set in Venice, *Othello* and *The Merchant of Venice*, are filled with references to Africa.

This project grew out of an astonishing line which appears late in Act IV of *Othello*. Othello has just visited Desdemona in

7

her bedroom and threatened her with terrifying and pointed menace. He leaves, and Desdemona, deeply shaken, asks her companion, Emilia, to help her get ready for bed. Entering an eerily emotional twilight that will lead to her violent death, she tells Emilia that she can't get a certain song out of her head. She learned this song, she tells Emilia, from her mother's maid, Barbary, who died while singing it, of a broken heart.

In one line, Shakespeare has suddenly given us a series of startling images. The appearance of the word "mother" tips us off – Shakespeare's plays are filled with mysterious, missing women and this is only the second reference to Desdemona's mother in the entire play. But it is the word "Barbary" which triggers surprising associations. In seventeenth-century London, "Barbary" meant Africa. The Barbary pirates were hijacking British vessels off the coast of Africa, enslaving their white, British crews. In 1600, a delegation of ambassadors from the Barbary court, Africans of high degree, splendidly dressed, arrived in London to negotiate with Queen Elizabeth. That advent stirred much discussion in London. That Shakespeare, writing *Othello* in 1603, uses the name "Barbary", implies that there is another African character in his play.

Shakespeare has already been at pains to demonstrate in Act I that Desdemona's parents don't know their own daughter, and now as she sings her famous "Willow Song," the quiet, dark, emotional still-point of the night, we are left to reflect that Desdemona – this tender, brilliant, courageous, generous young woman – was raised by an African maid with African stories and African songs. "Barbary" is one of Shakespeare's powerful and enigmatic "missing women" – he did not write for her, but he imagined her. In Toni Morrison and Rokia Traoré's *Desdemona*, we meet her at last, and Desdemona meets her again.

As a young woman, Desdemona rejected the usual suitors from the Venetian court – it was a black woman who taught Desdemona how to love and now, Desdemona chooses to offer her love to a black man. In Act I of *Othello*, Shakespeare has Othello tell the Venetian Senate that he and Desdemona fell in love as he told her stories – stories of his youth as a child soldier, stories of suffering, reversal, privation, salvation, transformation, and unexpected human generosity. Stories of "other worlds." And with the image of "Barbary" lingering in our minds, we can now imagine that Desdemona could have grown up hearing some of those stories.

And of course Toni Morrison wanted to write those stories.

In *Desdemona*, Toni Morrison has created a safe space in which the dead can finally speak those things that could not be spoken when they were alive. And finally, the women inside Shakespeare's play and those in the shadows, just outside of it, find their voices: Othello's mother and Desdemona's mother meet, and hidden histories are shared and begin to flow.

Desdemona was Shakespeare's ideal creation – like Dante's Beatrice, a vision of perfection, a woman offering love and forgiveness in the face of hatred, mistrust, and murderous lies. In Shakespeare's late tragedies, the ideal woman – Desdemona, Virgilia, Cordelia -- was mostly silent. For Toni Morrison, the ideal woman is not silent. Finally, she speaks. And as she speaks, she reveals secrets, hopes, dreams, but also her own imperfections. Shakespeare's Desdemona is divine perfection, but Toni Morrison allows her to be human, to make mistakes, and finally, with eternity stretching before her, to learn, and then to understand.

Shakespeare's play spans two days. Desdemona and Othello elope Monday night at 2 a.m., are thrust into a wild media-centric marriage as they travel in the public eye into a theater of war, and he has murdered her by Wednesday night. The play strangely offers no one much room for reflection. It is pointedly odd that the author of *Hamlet* affords the title character in *Othello* only a single twelve-line soliloquy. For the rest of the play, this black man is performing in front of white people and we have very few clues about his inner life. Desdemona is an astonishing teenager but is suffocated before she or we have a chance to learn her thoughts or feelings. In Toni Morrison's creation, Desdemona is no longer a teenager but a mature woman with perspective and the opportunity to gradually recognize and let go of her own illusions.

And so in *Desdemona*, we begin to glimpse some of the mysteries of Shakespeare's *Othello* with new insight in the light of deepened histories. What was the dark secret that held Othello and Iago in a bond of mutual dependency and hatred? What were the moments of happiness and promise and fulfillment in the great love between Desdemona and Othello before it was tainted by the world?

One other "silent woman" in Shakespeare's play enters into a new dimensionality: Emilia, Iago's terrified wife ("I nothing, but to please his fantasy."). She appears in nearly every scene of Shakespeare's play and she almost never speaks. She is the one person who knows the truth of the lie of the handkerchief – at any moment she could speak up and prevent the injustice and bloodbath that overwhelm the play.

Shakespeare creates a portrait of silence that is complicit with mass murder, that hopes by not uttering the truth to save its own skin, but that will in fact become the next victim when the lie follows its inexorable course.

Shakespeare's foil for Othello, the gifted, inspiring black leader, is Cassio, an ambitious, glib, weak career politician with a crippling addiction to alcohol and sex. Othello's first act as Governor of Cypress is to fire him, with cause. Desdemona, whose openness of spirit urges rehabilitation, redemption, and forgiveness, challenges her husband to reinstate Cassio, privately, and then in public. Shakespeare's mature tragedies strike a bitter note on their last page – the future will be even more bleak – after the flawed greatness of Hamlet we get Fortinbras. After Othello's death the terrible irony is that he is replaced as Governor by the mediocrity and venality of a wounded Cassio.

Toni Morrison responded to lacunae and poetic ambiguities in Shakespeare and to her own sense of unspoken truths. In communication with Toni by email, Rokia Traoré responded to Toni's unfolding story with songs that answered or deepened the human questions and the metaphysical aspects in an African context. Her work references African tropes and traditions. "Dongori" for example, refers to a woven cloth of thorns, a lament and an image that evokes a bitter African proverb for young women: your bridal veil will be your funeral shroud. In Rokia Traoré's new version, young women rewrite that proverb and defiantly, tenderly and respectfully claim a different future. The dah and kaicedrat in the overwhelming refrain of "Dianfa" are fruits with a pungent, acrid taste. The song "Kemeh Bourama" offers a brief sample of the centuries' old griot tradition. This is the way that the exploits of great warriors were recorded, sung and celebrated in the courts of Segou and Timbuktu, and we begin to hear the epic mode in which Othello's story would have been told in Africa in Shakespeare's lifetime.

In performance, dialogues spoken by the actress playing Desdemona are in dialogue with songs sung by Rokia Traoré as "Barbary". The only song lyrics not written by Rokia Traoré are Shakespeare's "Willow Song" and the pendant which Toni Morrison wrote in counterpoint to Shakespeare's "Willow Song," "Someone Leans Near."

Four hundred years later, Toni Morrison and Rokia Traoré respond to Shakespeare's *Othello*, offering some missing pieces and wider perspectives. Women now have the scope to speak their minds and their hearts, and Africa is real, not just imagined. The women speak to us from the other side of the grave, older now, no longer teenagers. In African traditions, the dead are quite undead and very present, and for them, as Toni Morrison says, the past and the future are the same. Desdemona and Othello meet again in the afterlife. With difficulty, humility and remorse, a space of reconciliation is created. The apologies that we have waited four hundred years to hear are finally spoken. We are not simply left with tragedy. In a time outside of time that illuminates and infuses the present, Des-demon-a confronts her "demons," reconciling the past, and now, no longer alone, prepares a future.

Peter Sellars
June 2012

Desdemona was commissioned and co-produced by Wiener Festwochen, Théâtre Nanterre-Amandiers, Cal Performances, Berkeley, California, Lincoln Center for the Performing Arts, New York, spielzeit'europa I Berliner Festspiele, and Barbican, London, Arts Council London and London 2012 Festival.

The premiere performance took place on May 15, 2011 at the Akzent Theater in Vienna, Austria.

Desdemona (Premiere)

Toni Morrison, Text

Rokia Traoré, Music and Barbary

Peter Sellars, Director

Elizabeth Marvel, Desdemona*

Mamah Diabaté, Ngoni

Fatim Kouyaté, Vocals

Bintou Soumbounou, Vocals

Naba Aminata Traoré Touré, Vocals

Mamadyba Camara, Kora

James F. Ingalls, Lighting Design

Alexis Giraud, Sound Design

Anne Dechêne, Production Stage Manager

Janet Y. Takami, Assistant Stage Manager

Diane J. Malecki, Producer

*Tina Benko in Nanterre, Berkeley, New York, Berlin and London

1.

DESDEMONA   My name is Desdemona. The word,
            Desdemona, means misery. It means ill
            fated. It means doomed. Perhaps my parents
            believed or imagined or knew my fortune
            at the moment of my birth. Perhaps being
            born a girl gave them all they needed to
            know of what my life would be like. That it
            would be subject to the whims of my elders
            and the control of men. Certainly that was
            the standard, no, the obligation of females
            in Venice when I was a girl. Men made the
            rules; women followed them. A step away
            was doom, indeed, and misery without relief.
            My parents, keenly aware and approving of
            that system, could anticipate the future of a
            girl child accurately.

            They were wrong. They knew the system,
            but they did not know me.

            I am not the meaning of a name I did not
            choose.

DESDEMONA

Small, uninhabited,

envious of manhood,

weakened.

You are unworthy of the femininity

that you haven't recognized in yourself,

that you distort,

that elevates and softens

your sad bitterness.

Though it feels strong,

beautiful and worthy,

we see your confusion,

sadness and hurt.

Mona, Desdemona

I exist in between, now: between being killed
and being un-dead; between life on earth
and life beyond it; between all time, which
has no beginning and no end, and all space
which is both a seedling as well as the sun it
yearns for. All that is available to me. I join
the underwater women; stroll with them
in dark light, listen to their music in the
spangled deep. Colors down there are more
violent than any produced by the sun. I live
in the roots and heads of trees. I rise in art,
in masks, in figures, in drumbeat, in fire.
I exist in places where I can speak, at last,
words that in earth life were sealed or twisted
into the language of obedience. Yes, my
Lord. By your leave, Sir.

If you had been a man
you could hardly have achieved more,
accomplished more.
Manhood in itself is not a plus.
Womanhood never imagined itself as an obstacle.
"Girl" does not know how to be less than "boy".
Together, they were chosen
to give meaning to life.

Is it a question of deciding
who is strongest?
Between He
who represents strength
and She
in whom all strength is rooted,
grows,
and is given meaning
and purpose?

Mona, Desdemona

Who is greater?
He, who claims supremacy
here below,
or She,
without whom there would be
no life
here below?

Mona, Desdemona

How can you confuse
finesse with obedience,
discretion with ignorance,
tenderness with submission,
seductiveness with prostitution,
woman with weakness?

Did you imagine me as a wisp of a girl?
A coddled doll who fell in love with a
handsome warrior who rode off with her
under his arm? Is it your final summation of
me that I was a foolish naïf who surrendered
to her husband's brutality because she had
no choice? Nothing could be more false.

It is true my earth life held sorrow. Yet
none of it, not one moment was "misery."
Difficulty, yes. Confusion, yes. Error in
judgment, yes. Murder, yes. But it was my
life and, right or wrong, my life was shaped
by my own choices and it was mine.

2.

My mother was a lady of virtue whose
practice and observation of manners were
flawless. She taught me how to handle myself
at table, how to be courteous in speech,
when and how to drop my eyes, smile,
curtsey. As was the custom, she did not
tolerate dispute from a child, nor involve
herself in what could be called my interior
life. There were strict rules of deportment,
solutions for every problem a young
girl could have. And there was sensible
punishment designed for each impropriety.
Constraint was the theme of behavior.
Duty was its plot.

I remember once splashing barefoot in
our pond, pretending I was one of the
swans that swam there. My slippers were
tossed aside; the hem of my dress wet. My
unleashed laughter was long and loud.
The unseemliness of such behavior in a
girl of less than one decade brought my
mother's attention. Too old, she scolded,
for such carelessness. To emphasize the
point, my slippers were taken away and I
remained barefoot for ten days. It was a
small thing, embarrassing, inconvenient, but
definitely clarifying. It meant my desires, my
imagination must remain hidden. It was as
though a dark heavy curtain enclosed me.
Yet wrapping that curtain over my willfulness
served to strengthen it.

My solace in those early days lay with my nurse, Barbary. She alone encouraged a slit in that curtain. Barbary alone conspired with me to let my imagination run free. She told me stories of other lives, other countries. Places where gods speak in thundering silence and mimic human faces and forms. Where nature is not a crafted, pretty thing, but wild, sacred and instructive. Unlike the staid, unbending women of my country, she moved with the fluid grace I saw only in swans and the fronds of willow trees. To hear Barbary sing was to wonder at the mediocrity of flutes and pipes. She was more alive than anyone I knew and more loving. She tended me as though she were my birth mother: braided my hair, dressed me, comforted me when I was ill and danced with me when I recovered. I loved her. Her heart, so wide, seemed to hold the entire world in awe and to savor its every delight.

Yet that same heart, wide as it was, proved vulnerable. When I needed her most, she stumbled under the spell of her lover. He forsook her and turned her ecstasy into ash. Eyes pooled with tears, she sang her loss of him, of love, and life.

M'BIFO

I thought that strength was in unity.
I thought that having you at my side
could keep me far from my solitude
and my fears

Now, I feel lost.
Now I know that love
can be a source of evil.
I love you.
I forgive you.

I forgot my solitude for a while.
I wanted to be with you, forever.
My outstretched hands waiting to be filled
are empty of disillusion.

My melancholy thoughts are back.
But I still love the idea of love.

Her spacious heart drained and sere, Barbary
died. I mourned her so deeply, it trembled
me. And yet, even in grief I questioned:
were we women so frail in the wake of
men who swore they cherished us? Was a
lover's betrayal more lethal than betrayal
of oneself? I did not know the answers, so
I determined to be otherwise. I determined
to search most carefully for the truth of a
lover before committing my own fidelity.
That determination was a blow to my father,
Senator Brabantio. His sole interest in me as
I grew into womanhood was making certain
I was transferred, profitably and securely,
into the hands of another man.

3.

With my father's invitations, and according
to his paternal duty, I was courted by many
men. They came into my father's house with
empty ornate boxes designed to hold coins
of dowry gold, or deeds of property. They
glanced at me and locked their glistening
eyes on my father's.

Showing their teeth in doting smiles they
slid in soft shoes on our marble floor. One
by one they came in velvet and fur-trimmed
silk, prettified hats stitched with silver thread.
Each one, whether a stuttering boy or an
aged widower, was eager for a chatelaine
weighted with riches. I was thought beautiful,
but if I were not, even if I were a giantess,
a miniature or a horse-faced shrew, suitors
cruising for a bride would have sought my
hand. Those already wealthy ranked me
with other virgins on their menu. Those in
desperate straits needed no evaluation.

My father instructed me on the virtues
of each offer and when I first refused he
thought me fastidious. With my next refusal,
he chastised me as stubborn; finally, as the
refusals continued, as an embarrassment: a
single female of a certain age, un-nunned,
sitting at his sumptuous table instead of
fasting in a convent.

I had reached the cusp of unmarriageability
– that lightless abyss into which a family can
fall – burdened by an eating mouth, tied to
a poor unseeded womb, disconnected from
the chain that the clan pays out to increase its
length and its profit.

Yet my flaw was more serious than pride.
It was revolt. I yearned for talk, for meaning,
for winds from a wider world. Seas beyond
canals, populations living other ways,
speaking languages of music and roar, beasts
and gods unimagined within these walls.
I longed for adventure out there, yes, but
inside as well. Adventure in my mind no less
than in my heart.

4.

One evening I veiled my surliness and
attended another of my father's endless
banquets.

Not yet recovered from Barbary's death, I
sat mute among the guests. Bountifully fed,
they began to dance – partnered, formal,
predictably flirtatious. Hoping to exit the
mockery, I stood and moved toward my
father to ask to be excused. Among those
huddled around his chair was this mass of
a man. Tree tall. Glittering in metal and red
wool. A commander's helmet under his arm.
As I approached, he turned to let me pass.
I saw a glint of brass in his eyes identical to
the light in Barbary's eyes. I looked away,
but not before his smile summoned my
own. I don't remember what I murmured
to my father to explain my approach. I was
introduced to the Commander; he kissed
my hand, held it and requested a dance. 'By
your leave, Senator Brabantio?' In accented
language his voice underscored the kiss.

We danced together, our bodies moving
in such harmony it was as though we had
known each other all our lives.

OTHELLO

By the grace of God
destiny smiles upon you.
The wishes of your grandparents
have been exalted and fulfilled.
Great Othello,
handsome Othello
only your anger
can make you lose
yourself.
Othello, a great man
does not give in to anger.
Contain your rage.
Let a river of peace
flow through you,
the serenity of a breeze
from the prairies.
Man should not make ugly
that which is beautiful
by the will of God.
No one should despise
what God wished to be desirable.
Do not allow the anger
to open in you
a fault that makes
your misfortune.
Othello, Othello
hold back your fury.
One does not destroy
what one loves.
One does not destroy
because one loves.

OTHELLO   Come to me Desdemona. Here on this bed
            let us make a world.

DESDEMONA   You will teach me?

OTHELLO   If you know how to laugh you will not need
            lessons. Desire is nature's purest gift.

DESDEMONA   And what is in this world we will make?

OTHELLO   Singing children watching men like me,
            warriors needing love, put down their swords
            to dance.

DESDEMONA   And women?

OTHELLO   Like you. With eyes than cannot hide
            the mind's sharp intelligence; a throat
            demanding my lips; shoulders inviting
            caresses; strawberry nipples hiding a bold
            and loving heart.

DESDEMONA   And laughter is our teacher?

OTHELLO   And our flesh is its lesson.

DESDEMONA   Then let my flesh be re-born through yours.

OTHELLO   Having captured glee, we melt and become
            one.

DESDEMONA   I adore you.

OTHELLO   I love you. Turn away old world, while my
            love and I create a new one.

5.

Two women approach each other. One is dressed in simple cloth, the other in a sumptuous gown. They both have white hair and carry a torch.

M. BRABANTIO   'Who are you?'

SOUN   'My name is Soun, and you?'

M. BRABANTIO   'I was Madam Brabantio in life.'

SOUN   'What brings you to this dark place?'

M. BRABANTIO   'I feel comfortable here. It suits me since I lost my daughter. And you? What brings you here?'

SOUN   'The same. I lost my son.'

M. BRABANTIO   'Who was he?'

SOUN   'A brave Commander named Othello.'

M. BRABANTIO   'Oh, no. Not he who murdered my daughter?'

SOUN   'Desdemona?'

M. BRABANTIO   'Yes.'

SOUN   'Are we enemies then?'

M. BRABANTIO   'Of course. Our vengeance is more molten than our sorrow.'

SOUN	'Yet, we have much to share. Clever, violent Othello.'
M. BRABANTIO	'Headstrong, passionate Desdemona.'
SOUN	'Both died in and for love.'
M. BRABANTIO	'Miserable. I prayed to Mother Mary for help when your son slaughtered my daughter.'
SOUN	'A waste. I spoke to my gods for guidance when, in remorse, my son responded with suicide.'
M. BRABANTIO	'Here are their graves. Let us kneel.'
SOUN	'Not yet. I come from a land wildly different from yours. A desert land pierced by forests of palm. There we obey nature and look to it for the language of the gods. We keep close the traditions they have taught us. One is our way of cleansing, of diluting the poisons life forces us to swallow.'
M. BRABANTIO	'And what is that way?'
SOUN	'An altar. We build an altar to the spirits who are waiting to console us.'

DONGORI
"Beautiful"
will be my plan.
Strong,
up to the task
and filled with pain.
Radiant,
I push back the hurt.
I harness myself
to every good thing
I can produce
whatever
my destiny.

Dongori,
violence.
Dongori,
obliteration.
Dongori,
enslavement.

Dongori,
I break the cord,
I undo the knot.

I free myself
from this vine of thorns.
At the heart of marriage
I grant myself
dignity
as my first
duty.

Today
I aspire to self-respect.
Mama,
do you understand me?
Today,
I aspire to self-esteem.
Papa,
will you forgive me?

6.

Who could have thought a military
commander, trained to let blood, would
be more, could be more, than a brutal arm
educated solely to kill?

I knew. How did I know?

We sat on a stone bench under an arch. I
remember the well of softness in his eyes.

And this is what he told:

OTHELLO   "As an orphan child a root woman adopted
                 me as her son and sheltered me from slavers.
                 I trailed her in forests and over sere as she
                 searched for medicinal plants, roots, and
                 flowers. She taught me some of her science.
                 How to breathe when there is no air.

                 Where water hid in cactus and certain vines.
                 She worshipped the natural world and
                 encouraged me to rehearse certain songs to
                 divine its power.

                 Yet soon I was captured by Syrians. I lived
                 with the camels and oxen and was treated
                 the same. I ate what I could find. It was
                 a happy day for me to be sold into an
                 army where food was regular and clothes
                 respectable. There I learned quickly the art
                 of arms and the strength of command. In
                 my first battle, I pointed my childish anger
                 with a daring completely strange to me. I
                 was happy, breathless and hungry for more
                 violent encounters. Only as a soldier could
                 I excel and turn the loneliness inside into
                 exhilaration."

And this is what he told:

OTHELLO "Our ship, upon an onslaught from land,
sank. I alone was able to swim ashore. As
I crawled along the beach I saw no enemy
waiting on a ridge above the white sand. But
I had heard the people of this place were
invisible. Others said they were not invisible
– they were chameleons able to assume
the shades they inhabited. They could be
detected only by their smell which meant
in order to encounter their odor, one had
to get close enough to be killed. I chose not
to discover which was true: invisibility or
camouflage. I knew there were tunnels in the
sea. If you walk the beach and listen carefully
you can hear the wind's music soughing
from a certain kind of rock or swirl of sand.
They signal an opening. Enter and a corridor
of light shines in front of you, a hallway as
dry as the Sahara, cool as the Himalayas. I
waited in the light of that sea tunnel three
days until the enemy believed me dead."

And this is what he told:

OTHELLO   "There is an island surrounded by a lavender ocean where fish leap into your boat, or you can reach into the waves and catch them in your hand; where trees bear fruit year round; where birds speak as humans; where the islanders have no heads and their faces are settled in their chests. Once, desperate for food and water, I was cast upon their shores. Although they laughed at my deformity, at the hilarity of my own head rising awkwardly and vulnerably above my shoulders, they were generous. They fed me and tended to my needs. All human attributes were theirs except for one: they could not sing for they had no throats. When I sang for them the songs the root woman had taught me, they crowded about. Tears rolled down to their waists as they wept their pleasure. It was difficult to sail away, so awed was I by their civilization."

And this is what he told:

OTHELLO   "There are armies of women who kill men
in battles so fierce the moon itself hides from
the ribbons of shed blood. They cut off their
right breasts to ease the arrow shots of their
long bows to lethal precision. For this they
are called No-Breast or A-Mazon and must
remain virgins until after the first time they
kill a man. With male blood they stain their
hair and with his bone they sharpen their
arrowheads. Whole regiments fall before
them. They rule wooded nations and desert
kingdoms. Waters and precious stones have
their names. I have seen them and marveled
at their war skills."

KEMEH BOURAMA

From your bloody battles
Dame Amazon,
could you bring me
the enemy's blood
so I can wash my face with it,
his intestines
so I can make a belt,
his skull
so I can make it
my throne?

The battle reaches its height.
Master of war
let your will be done.
Let his last victory be celebrated.
His victory over weakness,
cowardice, and mediocrity.
Let his courage be celebrated
here for the last time in his presence
and forever,
once he has been defeated
by what he has done.
The battle reaches its height.
Master of war
let your will be done.

And this is what he confessed:

OTHELLO   "Part, perhaps, most of the joy, the pleasure,
of battle I took as a child soldier came from
having comrades who were like me and who
loved the fresh green leaves we were given
to eat. Chewing them infused us with more
than courage: we were potent and indifferent
to blood, cries of pain, debasement – to life,
even our own. Rape was perfunctory. Death
our brother. It took capture, imprisonment
for months to be rid of the craving for the
leaves and to absorb what we had become.
The self loathing, however, could only be
quieted by the glint of honor an honorable
army provided. My acceptance into the
mighty forces of Venice was my salvation.
Since then, military justice coupled with
the virtue of the corps have guided me.
Your gaze, spilling pity and understanding,
embolden me giving me hope that this, my
secret, will be our bond."

Those are the tales he told. Tales that
stopped my heart as much as they fired
my mind. Tales of horror and strange. I
was captured by love and the prospect of
inhabiting a broad original world where I
could compete with the Amazons.

7.

My husband knew Iago was lying,
manipulating, sabotaging. So why did he
act on obvious deceit? Brotherhood. The
quiet approval beamed from one male
eye to another. Bright, tight, camaraderie.
Like-mindedness born of the exchange of
musk; the buck's regard of the doe; the mild
contempt following her capture. The wide,
wild celebrity men find with each other
cannot compete with the narrow comfort of
a wife. Romance is always overshadowed
by brawn. The language of love is trivial
compared to the hidden language of men
that lies underneath the secret language they
speak in public. But real love, the love of an
Amazon, is not based on pretty language or
the secret sharing between males.

Remember your last confession? The last tale
you told?

OTHELLO   Aroused by bloodletting, Iago and I entered
a stable searching for food or drink. What
we found were two women cowering. After
a first glance, they never looked at us again.
They lowered their eyes and whimpered.
They were old, so old. Fingers gnarled by
years of brutal work; teeth random and softly
withering flesh. No matter. We took turns
slaking the thirst of our loins rather than
our throats. I don't know how long it lasted.
Our groans and their soft crying drape my
memory of passing time. Once sated, we
heard a noise behind us coming from a

heap of hay. We turned to see a child, a boy, staring wild-eyed at a scene that must have seemed to him a grotesque dream. Except for the women's whimpering, silence fell.

DESDEMONA   Surely, surely you did not assault the boy. Tell me you did not.

OTHELLO   No. We never touched nor threatened him.

DESDEMONA   Then mercy triumphed, at last.

OTHELLO   Not mercy at all.

DESDEMONA   What then?

OTHELLO   There was a look between us. Before our decision to do no more harm our eyes met, Iago's and mine, in an exchange of secrecy.

DESDEMONA   And of shame?

OTHELLO   Shame, yes.

DESDEMONA   The unspeakable is no longer. Now you have pried loose the screws twisting your tongue. The telling is itself courage.

OTHELLO   You don't understand. Shame, yes, but worse. There was pleasure too. The look between us was not to acknowledge shame, but mutual pleasure. Pleasure in the degradation we had caused; more pleasure in leaving a witness to it. We were not only refusing to kill our own memory, but insisting on its life in another.

DESDEMONA	That is obscene, monstrous.
OTHELLO	Without question. Yet there is another question, a vital one. Can you forgive me?
DESDEMONA	No, I cannot. But I can love you and remain committed to you.
OTHELLO	In spite of what I have described?
DESDEMONA	In addition to what you have described. Did you think loving another was a profit-driven harvest: choosing the ripe and discarding the rot? Love is complete, whole, fearless; otherwise it is merely a banquet, a feast planned to sate a hunger for variety, not commitment to one choice. Honest love does not cringe at the first roll of thunder; nor does it flinch when faced with the lightning flash of human sin. I always knew you were caressing me with fingers hardened by swords and that your hands stroking my breasts also drew blood. My error was in believing that you were more than the visage of your mind.
OTHELLO	I pray I am more.

DIANFA

Do you know what torments me?
Do you want to know my anguish?
I fear the ultimate betrayal.
Will you abandon me?
Honey and sweetness
will never be separated.
Its acrid taste
remains faithful to the dah.
The kaicedrat will never lose
its bitterness.

Don't leave me.
My power is so frail
here below.
In one way or another
my time
is coming to
an end.

For me, old age
would be a pleasure.
I would destroy
whatever death might spare.
You are nothing more
than a game.
A game in which
I would still like
to take part.

Grant me the time I need
for wisdom
to grow in me
and give me the strength
to smile at my pain.
Don't leave me.
Honey and sweetness
will never be separated.
Its acrid taste
remains faithful to the dah.
The kaicedrat will never lose
its bitterness.

Stay with me
for the time it takes
for me to conquer my fears,
to overcome my agony.
You took back the substance
and the meaning you gave my life,
that rewarded my life.
Now, you abandon me
to nothingness.

8.

EMILIA	Well, well. If it isn't the martyr of Venice. Remember me? We died together. How do you do?
DESDEMONA	Emilia! I've wondered if I'd see you again.
EMILIA	Did you know I was the first to lay dying next to you?
DESDEMONA	All is known here, though not always understood.
EMILIA	What's left to understand? Both of us murdered, we failed. Noble as we tried to be, we failed.
DESDEMONA	Failed? As women? Emilia, you confound me. Didn't you acquiesce to all of Iago's demands, even the most vile, corrupt ones? Yet you admitted to me your willingness, eagerness even, to betray your own husband if it led to higher status. Your deception, your dangerous, murderous silence led to my death. And it led to yours.
EMILIA	Life is what it is. Women try to survive, since we cannot flourish.
DESDEMONA	I wonder if collapse of virtue is not survival at all but cowardice.
EMILIA	I resent that coming from one who had no defense against lies or her husband's strangling fingers.

DESDEMONA	And you, Emilia? You and I were friends, but didn't the man you knelt to protect run a gleaming sword through your survival strategies?
EMILIA	And why did he? Because I befriended and supported you. I exposed his lies, you ingrate! That is your appreciation for my devotion to you? "My cloak, Emilia," "My night gown, Emilia."
	"Unpin me, Emilia." "Arrange my bed sheets, Emilia." That is not how you treat a friend; that's how you treat a servant. Someone beneath you, beneath your class which takes devotion for granted.
DESDEMONA	It's true. I relied on your help and mistook it for benevolence. I was deceived.
EMILIA	You always thought me deceptive, simply because I would let myself be seduced in order to gain higher status. To own my life I had to forge a secret path.
DESDEMONA	Doesn't deception lead to ruin?
EMILIA	So does honesty, as your example shows. Like you I believed marriage was my salvation. It was not. Lust charged everything; satisfied itself everywhere; signaled by handkerchiefs; hid behind curtains. And all of that passion generated nothing. Not an infant among us. No progeny; no future. I was an orphan. I learned what I had to and polished those lessons daily. Otherwise the sorrow of motherlessness coupled with childlessness would have broken me.

DESDEMONA	Emilia, I wish I had known you when we were children. You had no family. I had too much. You had no mother. I had no mother's love.
EMILIA	It's not the same. An orphan knows how quickly love can be withdrawn; knows that complete safety is a child's hopeless dream.
DESDEMONA	You are right to correct me. Instead of judging, I should have been understanding.
EMILIA	Thank you for saying so. I am glad you never knew how desperate life is for the truly orphaned, our fear of losing our place. The long hours of servility in the grand halls of mistresses, the rush to hide from lascivious men – including your husband – the vulnerability, the ever-present danger. I stared at the moon for guidance, at the sea for answers.

They had none. Then, one day I saw a tiny lizard dozing in sunlight. Suddenly her scales seemed to move, to tremble. I watched as she shed her dull outer skin; struggled, then finally, crawled out of it, exposing that which had been underneath – her jeweled self. No one helped her; she did it by herself. What struck me, more than the brilliance of her new skin, was that she did not leave the outer one behind. She dragged it with her. As though the camouflage would still be needed to disguise her true dazzle. That little lizard changed my life.

9.

DESDEMONA	Barbary! Barbary. Come closer. How I have missed you. Remember the days we spent by the canal? We ate sweets and you saved the honey for me eating none yourself. We shared so much.
BARBARY	We shared nothing.
DESDEMONA	What do you mean?
SA'RAN	I mean you don't even know my name. Barbary? Barbary is what you call Africa. Barbary is the geography of the foreigner, the savage. Barbary? Barbary equals the sly, vicious enemy who must be put down at any price; held down at any cost for the conquerors' pleasure. Barbary is the name of those without whom you could neither live nor prosper.
DESDEMONA	So tell me. What is your name?
SA'RAN	Sa'ran.
DESDEMONA	Well, Sa'ran, whatever your name, you were my best friend.
SA'RAN	I was your slave.
DESDEMONA	What does that matter? I have known and loved you all my life.
SA'RAN	I am black-skinned. You are white-skinned.

DESDEMONA	So?
SA'RAN	So you don't know me. Have never known me.
DESDEMONA	Because of your skin? It is you who lack knowing. Think. I wed a Moor. I fled my home to be with him. I defied my father, all my family to wed him. I joined him on the battlefield.
SA'RAN	And he slaughtered you. Now do you know our difference?
DESDEMONA	And your lover slaughtered you as surely as if he had strangled you. Remember the song you sang every day until you wasted away and embraced death without fight or protest?

SA'RAN

> The poor soul sat sighing by a sycamore tree,
> Sing all a green willow;
> Her hand on her bosom, her head on her knee.
> Sing willow, willow, willow.
> The fresh streams ran by her, and murmur'd her moans;
> Sing willow, willow, willow;
> Her salt tears fell from her and soften'd the stones;
> Sing willow, willow, willow –

SA'RAN	Stop. Don't.
DESDEMONA	Listen to me.
SA'RAN	No, you listen. I have no rank in your world. I do what I am told. I brought you what you wanted before you knew you wanted it. I kissed your every cut and bruise. I held you when fever made you tremble, and when your parents made you weep. You never had to wash your hands or feet or face. I did that for you.
DESDEMONA	You blame?
SA'RAN	I clarify!
DESDEMONA	Sa'ran. We are women. I had no more control over my life than you had. My prison was unlike yours but it was prison still.
	Was I ever cruel to you? Ever?
SA'RAN	No. You never hurt or abused me.
DESDEMONA	Who did?
SA'RAN	You know who did. But I have thought long and hard about my sorrow. No more "willow". Afterlife is time and with time there is change. My song is new:

"Someone leans near
And sees the salt my eyes have shed.
I wait, longing to hear
Words of reason, love or play
To lash or lull me toward the hollow day.
Silence kneads my fear
Of crumbled star-ash sifting down
Clouding the rooms here, here.
I shore up my heart to run. To stay.
But no sign or design marks the narrow way.
Then on my skin a sudden breath caresses
The salt my eyes have shed.
And I hear a call – clear, so clear:
'You will never die again.'
What bliss to know
I will never die again."

DESDEMONA   We will never die again.

10.

DESDEMONA   Your cloak is tattered.

OTHELLO   So am I.

DESDEMONA   Why, may I ask?

OTHELLO   The endlessness of time and the depth of
regret equals hell.

OTHELLO   I always wanted to know why you stopped
struggling when I encircled your throat and
cut off your breath. Why did you let my rage
run free? Why did you deny I murdered
you?

DESDEMONA   You were not killing me. You were killing
Othello. The man I believed you to be was
lost to me. So what was left to struggle for?

OTHELLO   Tell me about this Othello you believed me
to be.

DESDEMONA   More than the rapture of his body; more
than the sword at his side. My Othello is not
the man who chose to believe what you must
have known was false.

OTHELLO   It's clear now. You never loved me. You
fancied the idea of me, the exotic foreigner
who kills for the State, who will die for the
State. Everyone I slaughtered was someone
who wanted your head on a pike. How
comforting it must have been – protected

by a loyal black warrior. What excited
you was my strange story: enslaved youth
ruined by war then redeemed by it, fantastic
adventures, stories of freaks and miracles.
A confession known only to you, my wife.
And you thought that was all there was to
me – a useful myth, a fairy's tale cut to suit
a princess' hunger for real life, not the dull
existence of her home.

DESDEMONA   You are wrong! You believed a lie. You broke
my hymen and thought I was unfaithful the
next day? Me?

OTHELLO   I don't know. I did suspect. Actually I don't
care. Listen to me. More than infidelity
my rage was toward your delusion. Your
requirements for a bleached, ultra-civilized
soul framed in blood, for court manners
honed by violence. Have you any idea
what it took to get to the position I held?
Who sabotaged me, delayed promotions,
took credit for my victories? Who fed
rumors about my intelligence, my virility,
my character? Even with the gore of their
enemies, the smell of it, the drips of it on my
sword, their contempt over-powered what
should have been glistening gratitude. Only
perseverance, discipline and a shrewd sense
of what truly matters kept me going. While
you played with my reality; toyed with it;
turned it into – into spectacle.

CASSIO interrupts.

CASSIO   Speaking of spectacle, I reckon it is superior
to a feeble reality, especially one that has
collapsed and become a barely controlled
nightmare. Those in charge of defending the

State slew one another like rival scorpions,
abusing their former comrades with deceit
and fury. But first came the poison of weak,
disloyal women. Fair Desdemona? Innocent
Desdemona? Hah! I have touched her
and she neither screamed nor slapped my
hands away. Then, to hurry the demise,
came that vain, arrogant Othello, swanning
about above his station and way above his
geography and his history. A dangerous
godless mix, unable to govern, to know
with certainty what is best for the State. I
am compelled now to repeal and replace
whatever they have initiated into law.

Dissolute. It's true. That is the word that
accurately describes my youth. Four liters of
wine I consumed before the sun touched the
top of heaven. Following its descent, well, I
couldn't tell anyone how much I drank. The
point is, it not only didn't interfere with my
duties, it helped me execute them. But when
I gave up brew, I was promoted by Othello;
then demoted by him. Why? I was tricked
into drunkenness! I relied too heavily on
my intimacy with Desdemona, hoping she
would make Othello give me back my job.
Then tricked again with the theft of a dirty
handkerchief. Finally wounded by the man I
believed my friend.

I acknowledge Othello was competent, even
intelligent. I understand he had vision. But of
what value is either in day-to-day rule? Who
needs vision to declare war and win it at all
costs? The needs of the State are mundane,
and therein safety lies.

The arrogance of that Moor riles me still.
Undermining him improves my status daily
and solidifies my power.

Now Cyprus is under my reign. I am the one
who decides. Othello gone from life; Iago
suffering in a prison cell. A clean sweep that
allows me to rule and perhaps help Venice
return to its prominence. Wars will be won,
not abandoned. Perhaps a stumble here and
there; some resisting voices of course, but
their subtlety will merely produce confusion.

So let me be clear. Power is more than
responsibility; it is destiny. Destiny few men
are able to handle. While there may be so-
called 'slaughter of the innocents' in its wake,
none of that will deter me. I bow, modestly,
to destiny's demands. Me alone. I am its
servant and it is mine.

DESDEMONA   To think I tried to save him. I was wrong, so
             wrong. Was Cassio always such a fool?

OTHELLO   Always. He enrages me as much now as he
             did then. But I hid my fury and overlooked
             his fatal ignorance because I believed him
             loyal. Fidelity is a necessity in the military.
             Lives depend on it, but I could not. I was
             doubted and deceived at every turn. Why?
             Because I am African? Because I was sold
             into slavery? Or because I was better than
             they? Whatever the reason, I had to prove
             myself over and over again. Cassio's fawning
             I welcomed in that malign atmosphere, until
             lies from every quarter infected me and
             disturbed the balance of my mind.

DESDEMONA	I apologize for a profound error in judgment.
OTHELLO	Apology is a pale word for what I am called upon to recognize. I am beyond sorry; it is shame that strafes me. And shame too for diminishing our life together as spectacle. It was never that.
DESDEMONA	True. Yet Cassio lives to rule and we do not because love cannot survive without trust.
	Your doubt and my righteousness mangled our love.
OTHELLO	We should have had such honest talk, not fantasy, the evening we wed.
	My love for you was mind deep.
	I murdered myself and you to stop the drama. If I could slay myself again, I would. But afterlife forbids a double death.
DESDEMONA	I am sick of killing as a solution. It solves nothing. Questions nothing, produces nothing, nothing, but more of itself. You thought war was alive, had honor and reason. I tell you it is well beyond all that. My mistake was believing that you hated war as much as I did. You believed I loved Othello the warrior. I did not.
	I was the empire you had already conquered.
	Alone together we could have been invincible.

OTHELLO   And now? Together? Alone? Is it too late?

DESDEMONA   'Late' has no meaning here. Here there is
only the possibility of wisdom.

Of knowing the earth is not quiet nor
waiting. In the screech of color and the
whisper of the lightless depths of the sea,
it boils, breaks or slumbers. And in this
restless rest human life is as unlimited and
miraculous as love. Here the infidel can
embrace the saint just as sunlight creates the
air we breathe.

KÉLÉ MANDI
When two beings meet,
each brings to the other a bit of themselves.
So we learn, we construct our selves, we evolve.
I bring what makes me different from you.
Give me a bit of what you are.
But do it with gentleness and tolerance,
since all that you impose upon me with force
will only leave the imprint
of your violence and your arrogance.
One can't force the other
to accept what is offered.
In accepting what you have to give,
I open you to what I have to offer.

DESDEMONA   The world is alive and even if we kill it, it returns fresh, full-throated and hungry for time and space in which to thrive. And if we haven't secured the passionate peace we yearn for, it is because we haven't imagined it. Is it still available, this human peace? In our privileged position in timelessness, our answer is a roar.

If it's a question
of working together
on the task,
I would be happy to take part.
Whether we are from the same place or not.
Whether we are from the same culture or not.
Should we celebrate this moment?
It would fill me with joy.

Must we discuss,
understand each other,
and decide?
I would be yours.
It would fill me with joy.
But for now,
while we talk,
I know that I can only shine
in the light of adversity
that opposes
my self
and my vices.

DESDEMONA   We will be judged by how well we love.

My pride,
my foolish pride in being human
disgusts me.
It is the source of so much evil.
I have no ambition to exist
in this world
except as an impermanent
element
facing eternity
with no choice
but to burn
then finish
one way
or another.

Toni Morrison

Toni Morrison was awarded the Nobel Prize for Literature in 1993. She is the author of many novels, including *The Bluest Eye*, *Beloved* (made into a major film), *Paradise* and, most recently, *Home*. She has also received the National Book Critics Circle Award and a Pulitzer Prize for her fiction. In addition to *Desdemona* her theatrical work includes writing the text for *Margaret Garner* (music composed by Richard Danielpour), and *Dreaming Emmett* an unpublished play directed by Gilbert Moses and performed at the Marketplace Capitol Repertory Theater of Albany. Ms. Morrison has written lyrics for Kathleen Battle (commissioned by Carnegie Hall), Sylvia McNair, Jessye Norman, and Andre Previn. Ms. Morrison founded the Princeton Atelier which for fifteen years has brought actors, composers, writers, and artists of all genres together to work with students on the artists' own projects. Several of her novels including *The Bluest Eye* have been adapted for the stage.

Rokia Traoré

Delicate, intense, and gifted with extraordinary presence, Rokia Traoré has created her own unmistakable style and sound, crafting a musical universe with deep roots in traditional Mali transformed by inspired, spontaneous elements of the avant-garde, rhythm and blues, and rock and roll. Daring and fresh, she moves, sings, and writes with a natural authority centered in serenity and strength. Her voice is timeless, inviting audiences into a profoundly personal emotional world, a dream, a trance, with surprising and delicious bursts of dance party energy. That illuminated mix of high spirits and meditative focus empower her to speak with courage and with grace about difficult topics, and power the momentum and determination that carries her music forward through deeply felt sadness into a realm that is visionary and healing.

First winning the Radio France International (RFI) *Discoveries Award* for Africa in 1997, the next year she was the revelation of the Festival Musiques Métisses d'Angoulême. By the time Rokia Traoré was 25, many leading African musicians, including the legendary Ali Farka Touré, recognized her as one of the great African voices of the future. Her first albums, *Mouneïssa, Wanita,* and *Bowmboï* (with guests ranging from Toumani Diabaté to the Kronos Quartet) are now classics. Her latest album, *Tchamantché,* took the French *Victoires de la musique* award for the best World Music album of the year 2009.

Her originality, innovation, and eclecticism have moved her beyond "world music" categories – she has always been adventurous in her choice of collaborators, creating refined and subtle cross-cultural projects with deep integrity, fineness of detail, and startling emotional precision. It was while working on a special commission for the 250th birthday of Mozart in Vienna's New Crowned Hope Festival curated by Peter Sellars in 2006, that she first met Toni Morrison. *Desdemona* reunites her with these colleagues several years later. In addition to her international touring and recording work, at home in Mali, she has founded the Passerelle Foundation devoted to supporting the next generation of Malian musicians.

Peter Sellars

Opera, theater, and festival director Peter Sellars is one of the most innovative and powerful forces in the performing arts in America and abroad. A visionary artist, Sellars is known for ground-breaking interpretations of classic works. Whether it is Mozart, Handel, Shakespeare, Sophocles, or the 16th-century Chinese playwright Tang Xianzu, Peter Sellars strikes a universal chord with audiences, engaging and illuminating contemporary social and political issues.

Sellars has staged operas at the Glyndebourne Festival, the Lyric Opera of Chicago, the Netherlands Opera, the Opéra National de Paris, the Salzburg Festival, the San Francisco Opera, and Teatro Real (Madrid), among others, establishing a reputation for bringing twentieth-century and contemporary operas to the stage, including works by Olivier Messiaen, Paul Hindemith, and György Ligeti. Inspired by the compositions of Kaija Saariaho, Osvaldo Golijov, and Tan Dun, he has guided the creation of productions of their work that have expanded the repertoire of modern opera. Sellars has been a driving force in the creation of many new works with longtime collaborator composer John Adams, including *Nixon in China*, *The Death of Klinghoffer*, *El Niño*, *Doctor Atomic*, and *A Flowering Tree*. A staging of their latest work, *The Gospel According to the Other Mary*, will be seen in the U.S. and Europe early in 2013.

A Harvard graduate, Sellars was appointed Artistic Director of the American National Theater at the John F. Kennedy Center for the Performing Arts in Washington, D.C. at the age of 26, where between

1984 and 1986 he originated seven productions and presented eighteen others from a wide range of American and international theater companies. His landmark ANT staging of Sophocles' *Ajax*, set at the Pentagon, was invited to tour Europe and ignited the start of an international career. Other noteworthy theater projects include a 1994 staging of Shakespeare's *The Merchant of Venice* set in southern California with a cast of black, white, Latino, and Asian-American actors; an Antonin Artaud radio play coupled with the poetry of June Jordan, *For an End to the Judgment of God/Kissing God Goodbye*, staged as a press conference on the war in Afghanistan; a production of Euripides' *The Children of Herakles*, focusing on contemporary immigration and refugee issues and experience; and, in 2009, *Othello*, inspired by and set in the America of newly elected President Barack Obama.

Desdemona, Sellars' collaboration with the Nobel Prize-winning novelist Toni Morrison and Malian composer and singer Rokia Traoré, was performed in Vienna, Brussels, Paris, Berkeley, New York, and Berlin in 2011, and presented in London as part of the 2012 Cultural Olympiad.

Sellars has led several major arts festivals, including the 1990 and 1993 Los Angeles Festivals; the 2002 Adelaide Arts Festival in Australia; and the 2003 Venice Biennale International Festival of Theater in Italy. In 2006 he was Artistic Director of New Crowned Hope, a month-long festival in Vienna for which he invited international artists from diverse cultural backgrounds to create new work in the fields of music, theater, dance, film, the visual arts, and architecture for the city of Vienna's Mozart Year celebrating the 250th anniversary of Mozart's birth.

Sellars is a professor in the Department of World Arts and Cultures at UCLA and Resident Curator of the Telluride Film Festival. He is the recipient of a MacArthur Fellowship, the Erasmus Prize, the Sundance Institute Risk-Takers Award, and the Gish Prize, and is a member of the American Academy of Arts and Sciences.